# That Thread Still Connecting Us

# That
# Thread Still
# Connecting Us

*Joseph Green*

MoonPath Press

Poetry

ISBN 978-1-936657-03-2

Cover art by Eric Zimmer

Design by Tonya Namura
using Californian FB

MoonPath Press is dedicated to
publishing the best poets of the U.S. Pacific Northwest

MoonPath Press
PO Box 1808
Kingston, WA 98346

MoonPathPress@yahoo.com

http://MoonPathPress.com

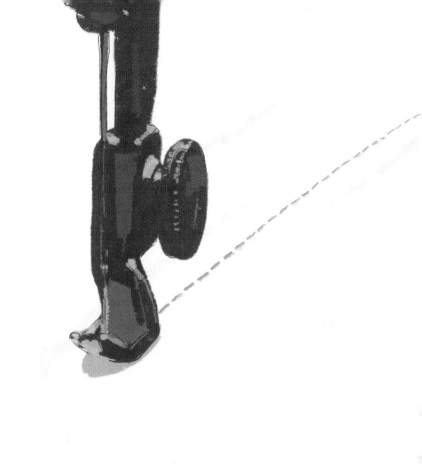

# Acknowledgments

Deep gratitude to the editors of the publications where these poems previously appeared, many in somewhat different versions:

Cooweescoowee: "Pasture with Black Horses Running."

Crab Creek Review: "Glasses," "Needle" (as "The Needle"; reprinted with the abbreviated title in Floating Bridge Review #4), and "Recliner."

5 AM: "Jesus, Charles Manson" (as "Jesus, You Look Like Charles Manson"; reprinted with the abbreviated title in Pontoon #10), and "The Shoes."

Hipfish: "Afternoon in the Plaza."

How to Be This Man: The Walter Pavlich Memorial Poetry Anthology (Swan Scythe Press): "Among the Potsherds."

Nimrod International Journal of Poetry and Prose: "A Postcard from Salamanca" and "Sweating Copper."

Slipstream: "Someone to Watch Over Me."

The Threepenny Review: "My Granddad's Last Career" (reprinted in Greatest Hits, 1975-2000, Pudding House Publications).

Vox Populi: "Dostoevsky."

Willow Springs: "The Catch" (reprinted in Line Drives: 100 Contemporary Baseball Poems. Brooke Horvath and Tim Wiles, eds. Southern Illinois University Press).

The epigraph to "A Postcard from Salamanca" is from the poem "Gesto final," in I'm Speaking: Selected Poems, by Rafael Guillén, Hydra Books, Northwestern University Press, 2001.

Special thanks to Kevin Miller, Allen Braden, and Derek Sheffield, who commented on many of these poems in their early drafts. Let's pick it up, boys, and do it again.

# Contents

*For Marquita:*
*This thread, too.*

# That
# Thread Still
# Connecting Us

# Needle

My mother had a black Singer
sewing machine when I was very young.

It chugged along, making straight seams
like a stationary train engine spitting out track

or if I squinted just right I felt like I was
riding in a car, looking out the back window,

watching telephone wires swoop away
pole to pole along the shoulder of the road.

Once, entranced by the way it pumped,
I reached my finger up to touch

the thin bright shaft,
the part I loved best,

and now I can't look
a needle in the eye

without thinking of that thread
still connecting us.

# Glasses

I was four years old when I broke
my first pair,

having fallen asleep with them on,
having then rolled over.

Whatever my mother said after that
I couldn't swallow.

It stuck to my tongue,
it dissolved there, bitter as aspirin tablets.

Whatever my father said was medicine as well,
intended, I'm certain, to cure me early

of my carelessness,
my irresponsibility.

I thought by now those pills would all be gone.
I thought I surely would have thrown them away,

but today when I tried to name
my first memory, it was still

the brittle snap of those plastic frames,
sharp as a mirror cracking,

an alarm waking me
again into the blurry world

where I knew I'd done something wrong,
something I might not ever grow out of.

# Oklahoma, Mon Amour

Saturday, my sister telephones, asking
whether I remember how our mother,

gone from Shawnee more than forty years,
began to speak with a noticeable twang

again in the last days before she died.
I say No, to me she only sounded tired.

That isn't what my sister wants to hear,
but it's a cold morning, winter hanging on

into spring, small hail ticking against
the kitchen window, covering the driveway

where my truck is parked, its windshield
as foggy under the slush as my recollection

of Stillwater: how fist-sized
ice balls once pounded Dad's Pontiac

until he had to pull over beside a big willow.
He said he was sure we'd be

all right.  He turned the knob
on the radio and tuned-in Howdy Doody,

hailstones still hammering
the roof, hood, trunk lid.

Still splattering all over the street.
Carpeting the neighborhood lawns

between me and my sister, safe
at home. Her long-distance

voice here in my kitchen now.
I can't tell you what she's been

talking about, but I catch myself
saying Yes, of course. Exactly.

# The Keeper of the Flame

My sister says we had a Pontiac then,
blue with white-sidewall tires, plastic
spinner knob on the steering wheel.
Our parents were both wearing hats,
his with the brim curving down in front,
up in back like a gray felt wave, the fine
spray of her white veil spilling over her face.
My sister thinks I wouldn't have seen them

leaving. But it's coming back now, I say.
The hats and the hood ornament, translucent
chief in his war bonnet, all those chrome
feathers blown back. Speed in his teeth.
I want to know why she didn't stop them.
I want to know if she said anything at all.
She says she never asked questions back then.
She says they knew what they were doing.

# 1014 West 4th Street

Fifty years later, I found the house
down, flattened by a parking lot,
someone's Toyota where the kitchen
sink had been, then two empty spaces,
and a blue pickup in my bed. The elm tree
in the grassy strip between the sidewalk and the street
looked a little ragged, as if it had just gotten up
one morning and found itself jobless, nothing
to stand in front of, and no one around to remember
what happened the day we left: Daddy loading
the trailer, nesting chairs together over suitcases,
over cartons of dishes, books—and Granddad
shoving him back, taking a swing at him
on the front porch when he tried to go in
for another load, my sister and I
watching from behind the tree as they leaned
into one another, grunting and clutching,
shouting themselves out of breath.
Staggering under the weight of something
neither one of them was ever going to drop.

# My Granddad's Last Career

Not one of his wristwatches
ever kept time after he'd fixed it,
although he eventually did get one to tick,

its flat hands jerking like nerve
damage, like delirium tremens,
around its white, innocent face.

# Someone to Watch Over Me

Months after Granddad died he still hung
around in the hall outside my room,
keeping an eye on me the way he'd always done.

I accused him of spying when he was alive,
when I caught him four or five times a day
easing my door ajar and peering inside.

Get your nose out of my business, I hissed,
and the door sucked shut and he slipped
back down the hall, but then after he was gone

there was no more getting rid of him.
My mother gave all his clothes away,
the pinstriped suits, the hats, the underwear,

and scrubbed the smoke stains out of his room
and sold his bed, his dresser, and his easy chair.
But I could still feel him sneaking up behind me,

distracting me from my algebra,
from the unknowns I had to isolate
among the numbers I couldn't love,

his breath whistling soft as cotton through his nostrils,
the invisible gift of his attention lifting
the hairs on the back of my neck.

That was the winter I first sipped liquor
and first sniffed a girl on my slippery finger.
That was the winter I learned what it is to be haunted.

# The Catch

Under a high fly ball to right
a boy runs in, calling *I got it*,
then changes his mind and backpedals.
No place anywhere is lonelier than right field now.

Half the parents in the bleachers pray for him
to get this one; then the other half give thanks
for what happens. The ball squirts up from the web
of his glove, a trout leaping out of water's grip,

and in the suspended moment before it falls
back into gravity's lap, it hangs over the boy
like an insult, so hard and spherical that he can't
even hear what everyone around him is shouting.

# Sweating Copper

My father taught me the hard way:
dusty coveralls in the crawl space

with the water off, and no matter what,
we were stuck there until we finished up.

Cobwebs strung the floor joists
where I had to aim the trouble light

and hold it still so he could see
just what the hell was going on.

If I let it slip, he grabbed my wrist
and dragged the light back where he wanted it

above the tubing cutter and the emery cloth
and the little metal-handled flux brush

in the jar of flux. The solder wire
coiled around itself the way I wrapped

my thoughts on their hollow core.
Then the quiet hiss of bottled gas,

flint-scratch of the spark lighter,
the blue tongue licking through the flame

along the copper pipe to make the solder run
bright as mercury into the fitted seam.

Smell of cool dirt. Smell of coffined air.
Smell of gas and flux and solder vapor

piercing it all like my father's whisper:
*Can't you pay attention, maybe, just for once?*

# Jesus, Charles Manson

That hair, he said, that hair
and that beard and that look
in your eye, he said, and that hair
and that trash on your tongue
and that beard and those filthy jeans,
he said, I wonder just what you think
I see when I see you, he said,
with that hair and that beard
and that look in your eye and
those filthy jeans and that trash
on your tongue, he said, and by now
he was shouting, that greasy hair
and that beard and those filthy jeans
I mean Jesus, he said, you look like
Charles Manson with that greasy hair
and that beard and that look in your eye
and those trashy jeans and that
filth on your tongue and that look
and that trash and that filth
and that hair and that beard
and those jeans I mean Jesus,
he said, I mean Jesus.

# The Boats in the Harbor

Within an hour after I left her ICU bedside
my mother stopped breathing and her heart
quit and the IV drip had nothing more to do
and the monitor rang for room service and
someone came to turn it off but that was not me

because I was eating breakfast in Trinidad
at a restaurant overlooking the harbor
where a fishing boat emerged from the fog
like a dim thought forming itself into an idea.
My father had said Mom needed to rest

after the operation and I should eat something
before I started the long drive north. He liked
this restaurant. He was picking up the check.
Neither of us would ever see my mother
again after that but we didn't know it at the time.

Seagulls wheeled up from their sullen posture
on the dock to greet the boat with a noisy chorus
of sharp cries and squawks. Critics everywhere,
I said, meaning the way the birds received this
newly formed idea, but my father didn't get it.

To him the seagulls were simply hungry
seagulls, and the boat was only a white trawler
with a wide blue stripe above the rubstrake
where the crew had hung a collection of bright orange
fenders to take up the impact of coming home.

# Dostoevsky

One winter the basement flooded
and mice invaded the kitchen, so I laid

baited traps in the lower cabinets
and waited.  Back then, I worked all day

stringing rafters, framing the roofs
of houses I couldn't imagine buying,

then stopped on the way home to drink
a pitcher or two with friends at the tavern

and pick up a six-pack to finish after dinner.
I liked cooking, but I wasn't so big

on washing dishes. Usually I just left them
stacked up in the sink.  I'd been reading

*The Brothers Karamazov*, pushing a little farther
into it each night—feet on the hearth, a blanket

around my shoulders, the house cold as Moscow—
and when the first mouse found the cheese

I was half asleep.  I might have missed the sound
of the wire snapping down on his neck

if the kill had been clean, but it wasn't.
In fact, it took that mouse a good ten minutes

to die.  I don't remember where I was
in *The Brothers Karamazov*, but the mouse

was in the empty cereal drawer,
flopping around, rattling the platform

of his trap against the walls and floor
of the dark, little room he had crept into,

looking, I guess, for something better than what he had,
something he might use to improve his situation.

# Still Life with Pioneer Grandmother

When her long-dead uncle
left the homestead near Meeker
to appear in my leather jacket and jeans,
my red Ché Guevara tee-shirt,
shaggy beard and hair, right there
beside her hospital bed, she said,
Why, Uncle Johnny!  How you been?

Light dropped across her sheets from the window,
and someone rattled a dinner cart down the hall,
and I, who had never spent a minute working
on anybody's farm, said Mighty fine.
I said we'd had mild weather, the hay
was finally in, and everybody hoped
she would be joining them soon.

# The Shoes

The night I hauled my father down
to emergency I had to get him dressed first.
It was about as simple as greasing up a snake
and sliding it back into the dry skin it had split out of
or forcing a whole live pig into a sausage wrapper.
Something in him wouldn't be compressed.

On my way to his apartment I'd passed a lost Cadillac
hubcap, and I'd taken it
as a sign, someone's mark, even there
on the meaningless shoulder of the road.
I thought of my father's flamboyant signature
staking out the territory at the bottom of a promissory note.

But when I found him cowering in bed with the shakes
and saw his shoes lined up like suspects
along his bedroom wall, all of them
polished, heels touching the baseboard,
I knew every pair of them had been somewhere
I didn't even want to think about going.

# The Stoma

*Mouth*, it means.
It needs attention. *Look at me
now*, it demands,

knotted red blossom
on my father's belly where
surgery has turned his intestine

through the wall.  It spits
whenever it feels like spitting,
drools as the spirit moves it.

Just when I have peeled away
the soiled pouch, cleaned
his skin, prepared

a new attachment patch,
the stoma spills a brown
mouthful of soup

into my father's crotch. His hands
jerk, leap, unlikely puppets
on someone else's strings.

He isn't himself today, he says.
Skin sagging, color wrung out,
he sinks behind his quiet disguise,

too dignified to say what he is
feeling. First the damp washcloth,
then the alcohol swab again,

but just as I fix a fresh pouch
into place, the stoma sputters
a wet fricative, one long raspberry.

It never gives in: pinched
little critic, pursed lips. No one
is ever going to kiss it.

# Recliner

One head, talking bloody murder,
turning on its neck, nods solemnly,
and the camera follows, pans
to another head, also bobbing
but far too perky for these circumstances.

What my father sees: a pretty face
framed by his slippers, his bony,
blue-pajamaed knees.  She says,
Coming up, the love life of sea lions!
*Don't go away!* Camera zooms out,

frames both heads, both smiling
like toothpaste ads. No news is good,
so Dad thumbs his remote toward
more impossible teeth, tiny women
spinning, their feet laced into skates.

Either that or he sleeps. No commercial
breaks, just weather changing, then
changing again. Every day pretty much
the same. Reruns running in his
mental theater. Elaborate staging,

the covert treachery of abandonment,
all done in the wings. What my father
sees: these scheduled visitations. Events
leaping, lurching away while his lost pocket-
knife turns up again or his car keys jingle

on memory's ring. Or this is somebody
else's television, someone else's head
talking stock market and whatnot,
all of it remote, all of it gone now
or else still going out of his control.

# A Postcard from Salamanca

*Esto es lo más terrible de los muertos:*
*que la vida los cubre y los absorbe.*

. . . . . . . . . . .

*Y esto es lo más terrible de los muertos:*
*que se paran de pronto entre las cosas.*
                    –Rafael Guillén, "Gesto final"


Frog squatting on a human skull,
        the skull carved in the stone façade
of the university where Fray Luis de León
        once taught, who spent five years in jail
for the crime of taking the Song of Solomon
        from Latin to *castellano*.
Who, upon his release, is said to have begun
        his next lecture, *As we were saying*
*yesterday* . . . The benches where his students
        concentrated or nodded off
or dug their names into the wood
        nearly five hundred years ago,
still there. I thought my father, old professor,
        might want to know I'd seen the way
patience seems to linger in such a place,
        how sense persists.
But the card I meant to send from Salamanca
        said, *I'll probably see you before you read this.*


Postcard on the hotel nightstand, clothes
        in a heap on the chair, I woke early,
and in the shower's hot water I thought
        again of my father: the way

he would always wait for me
        to rub him down with his towel,
the way he would grip the chrome safety
        bar with both hands, dripping,
enduring those moments. Bent image
        in his mirror, kinked fingers, fierce
tremor, crooked spine. And in that steam-filled room
        I knew right then
he would never read the card I had written.
        Washed in the noise of Spanish TV news,
I rushed downstairs to retrieve e-mail
        and found two messages saying my father
had fallen, he was all but gone.

What remains so important for the living
        to do? I drifted downtown
with the pedestrian river, eddying around
        every shop entrance, every window,
my reflection sliding over whatever was in it—
        shoes, soccer balls, Spanish hams, olives,
tourist junk, tee-shirts, *recuerdos de Salamanca*—
        until I ran aground, bought
a black decal of the frog squatting on a skull,
        emblem of human failing,
or good luck if you could find it
        in the wall where it was carved.
My luck? My father was dying—*As we were*
        *saying yesterday*—his sentence interrupted.
In restaurant windows people ate and drank,
        apparently feeling what they were

supposed to feel. Caught in the same glass,
     I floated past them

on my father's vast absence,
     a final gesture, a last kiss
folded in the wallet of my loss.
     In my pocket, the postcard's river
repeated trees, a single cloud and blue sky
     on water still as patience, making sense,
pausing at a weir before it spilled over, white,
     the city behind it—peaked roofs, tiles,
cathedral spires, stone on stone—standing its ground.
     Is it safe to say *relief* now? Old wall,
my father down, and no more carving on him?
     Whatever built or broke him, done?
Intricate façade all finished and worn away?
     Gone to sand? I am not sorry.
What pulled me from my room that morning
     could have been simple coincidence,
but I took it as a signal,
     the very moment he let go,

took it as a gift, his finally giving up.
     His stopping so suddenly
in the midst of events, letting others
     cover him, take him in—the most
terrible thing—*lo más terrible de los muertos.*
     But also the most forgiving,
forgivable, this helplessness,
     this interrupted moment—

what remains so important
        for the living—how it simply ends.
The most terrible thing about the dead?
        No one left to send or receive the mail.
No one there to witness
        what my father said, at last.
Terrible, how no one saw him
        climbing out of bed,
how no one finally caught him, falling.
        How no one picked up the lecture—

*As we were saying yesterday*—when
        I came home to his closet
and hauled his empty clothes away.
        I boxed the postcard from Salamanca
along with his other correspondence.
        What remains, after all,
so important for the living?
        Is it safe to say *relief*? What I keep,
what I cannot give away—that moment,
        that interruption, when I knew
my father was beyond my saving him—
        is my only souvenir.
Its emblem on the back window of my truck,
        the frog squatting
atop a human skull, my black luck,
        now follows me in the rearview mirror,
no matter where I might be driving.

# Among the Potsherds

When I climbed the hill
where the ancient city had been,
I didn't know what to expect
so I didn't expect anything. Certainly not
a cistern dug into the top, long ago gone dry,
its plastered stone walls finally caving in.
The ground around it littered with bits
of crockery. Ordinary lives.
Ambitions spilling. Plans failing.
Dreams seeping out through the cracks.
I picked up a shard from the lip of a water jar.
None of the other fragments appeared to match it.
Then I knew among these people I would have been
the same as I was at that moment. Wanting
to remain completely alone and whole.
Wishing I could go to pieces, even so.

# Afternoon in the Plaza

Shadows of palms, shadows
of olive trees, heat leaking out of the day
through the holes they make.

I've found an empty bench in the shade,
away from the other men strolling
in pairs or threes or fours, their hands

clasped behind their backs,
opinions hovering in front,
leading them on. Someone's dog

has gotten loose and jumped
into the fountain and now has leaped out again.
I think this must be the way

I think: one idea making a splash,
then trotting off like a wet dog, paw prints
lingering until the next thought crosses them

and is also gone.  I'm certain I ought to be
doing something, but I don't know what.
I might sit right where I am until after dark.

# A Place for Everything and
## Everything in Its Place

The spray-painted silhouettes of hammers, handsaws,
pipe wrenches, pliers on the pegboard wall, the tools
themselves sprayed yellow—this was my father,
imposing order in the college theater scene shop
where he taught.  At home, he built his own workbench
with slots, cradles to match tool handles and blades
so each chisel, each plane could fit only one way.
At least that was the plan. In practice,
the Phillips screwdriver took off with the socket wrench,
and the son-of-a-bitching center punch simply
disappeared. It had been *right here*, right where
he had set it down, and then it wasn't. That's how I felt

whenever I saw my students away from school.
I couldn't begin to remember their names.
And walking home from my office on a full-moon night,
I cut across the wet grass of the church yard and startled
a herd of elk grazing by the playground fence. They bolted,
more than a dozen of them, into blackberry shadows.
I couldn't say how they'd found their way this far into town,
but each morning after that I looked for signs: hoof marks
chopped into the lawn, shiny black clumps of shit,
scattered pebbles of it leading to muddy paths
nearly hidden behind these houses, these orderly yards
with their swing sets, their flower beds, their
    cultivated gardens.

# Ivory

When someone recorded what might have been
its distinctive hammering, its high-pitched wild cry,
ornithologists flocked into Arkansas, all searching for the bird
so shocking it had come to be called The Lord God—
whom you cannot claim to know without diminishing Him,
though you may find indelible signs wherever you look.
And today I have spent all morning looking

for a white elephant carved from a chunk of tusk
small enough to fit the palm of a child's hand.
My aunt brought it home from India before the war
and gave it to my father, who stored it in his sock drawer.
Tucked in among the matched black pairs, it was,
for me, the cool, smooth cream of longing,
which now I see is all that's left
after everything else is gone.

# Pasture with Black Horses Running

Headlong—the right word
for their rushing to the fence,
their wheeling away from it,
the first ones, and the ones behind
peeling off after them, then racing
back across the pasture,
dirt flung up in clumps, and dust
hanging, stunned, where they turned
and galloped out from under it.
I couldn't hear the hard thumping
of their hooves, their breath rasping
the air outside my car, windows rolled
up and radio playing, but there they were,
black locomotive of driving legs,
whipping tails and manes, all of them
almost tumbling headfirst, maybe
longing to break out, run
farther, faster, and I caught myself
giving thanks for the fence, its thin
threat of electric shock the only thing
keeping the horses from pouring out
over the road, my car speeding past
as they spun away, narrow pavement
aiming straight where I was
supposed to be going.

# Driving Alone

Tight between dry ditches, flat fields,
the two-lane highway runs straight as the blue
chalk line my father would push his saw along

to divide a plywood panel into manageable
pieces. Ashes, ashes all fallen down, he's still
telling me what's what. I'm still turning the radio up.

## About the Author

Joseph Green lives in Longview, Washington, where he taught at Lower Columbia College for twenty-five years. His poems have been appearing in magazines and journals since 1975, and many are collected in *His Inadequate Vocabulary* (The Signpost Press, 1987), *Deluxe Motel* (The Signpost Press, 1991), *Greatest Hits: 1975–2000* (Pudding House, 2001), and *The End of Forgiveness*, which won the Floating Bridge Poetry Chapbook Award for 2001. He designs and prints limited-edition letterpress poetry broadsides through The Peasandcues Press, in partnership with his wife, Marquita. At the C.C. Stern Type Foundry in Portland, Oregon, he draws on his experience from the Hill & Dale Foundry's "Monotype University," where he participated in a casting of *Californian*, Monotype's 1958 public reissue of *California Old Style*, the face that Frederic W. Goudy cut in 1938 for the University of California Press. *Californian FB*, used throughout this book, is the digital version of the Monotype face.

Made in the USA
Charleston, SC
04 January 2012